From My Heart and Spirit to Yours

A Collection of Poetry

William H. Lewis, III

Copyright © 2020 by William H. Lewis, III
Los Angeles, California
All rights reserved
Printed and Bound in the United States of America

Published by
OliWill Publishing
Los Angeles, California 90062
Email: lewisbilll1030@gmail.com

Cover design: TWA Solutions
First printing: February 2020
978-1-7344901-0-7
10987654321

No part of this book may be reproduced, stored in a retrieval system or transmitted in any form or by any means without the prior written permission of the publisher—except by a reviewer who may quote brief passages in a review to be printed in a newspaper, magazine or journal.

For inquiries contact: lewisbilll1030@gmail.com

Acknowledgments

To my rock, best friend, and the best mother in the world, my awesome wife, Cynthia. Thank you, babe, for always believing in me, and allowing me to be the man that God created me to be. I love you unconditionally.

To our beautiful children, Olivia and William; Daddy loves you more than words can express. You push me more than you'll ever know. Always know that you can do all things through Christ Jesus.

To my amazing parents, Mr. William Lewis Jr. and Ms. Ann Lewis. Mom and Dad, you are the greatest teachers of life, and I have learned so much by observing, listening, and taking notes. You are the epitome of resilience and perseverance. Thank you for passing it down.

And to the great memory of my wonderful and amazing sister, Ms. Natasha L. Lewis. Natasha, thank you for molding, nurturing, shaping, loving, supporting, and helping me become the best man I can be. I will love you forever, Natasha, and may you rest eternally with God.

From My Heart and Spirit to Yours

A Collection of Poetry

The Almighty God

God woke you up this morning,
God watched over you.
God loves you unconditionally,
God kept you in the midst of the storm.
God blessed you despite your unworthiness,
God fed you when you were broke,
God covered you when you were naked.
God delivered you from alcohol,
God delivered you from drugs,
God cried with you during your darkest hours,
God carried you when you were lost,
God continued to love you, despite your evil ways.
God brought you out of the dungeon,
God comforted you,
God gave you wisdom,
God gave you understanding.
God gave you direction,
God gave you light to dispel the darkness,
God don't need your help.
God wants you to have faith in Him,
God is all that we need.
God is everything,
God is, and always will be, your first love.

Human

I'm humiliated daily.
Called bad names and disrespected.
My bed is made of concrete.
My bed gets cold at night.
I try my best to stay warm.
I can't get comfortable.
I hear loud noises all through the night.
I compete with the rats and the birds for food.
The rats and the birds eat better than me;
The rats and the birds are ruthless.
I can't take it anymore.
Where will I go?
I have no one to call.
I'm stuck here.
People walk past me but fail to acknowledge my presence.
There are those rare occasions when I encounter an empathetic being.
I often wish that my life was better.
I get very lonely.
I'm always hungry.
Please bring me something to eat.
Please bring me some clean clothes.

From My Heart and Spirit to Yours: A Collection of Poetry

Please direct me to a shower.
Please help me to regain my dignity,
Please tell the police that I'm harmless.
I have feelings, too.
I cry frequently.
I am tired of living.
God wakes me up every day.
My life has purpose
Please pray for me.

Rage

He cheated on me.
She degraded me.
They disrespected my mother.
She slapped my daughter.
My pay check is never enough.
They treated me differently.
He shot my brother.
I got harassed by the police.
I missed the bus three times this week and my boss wrote me up.
I lost my job.
My husband spends money on prostitutes.
My wife spent the rent money on shoes and clothes.
They did not let me out of jail to attend my grandmother's funeral and she raised me.
My sister was sexually assaulted.
My son was molested.
My wife got pregnant by another man.
My teacher called me stupid.
My parents got deported.
Our slumlord raised the rent last month.
Somebody broke in my car and stole my battery.
I have three degrees and still can't find a job.

The Great Beacon

My brother, I give you all of the love and respect that you so deserve.
The beginning of your journey was rough, tough, and downright ridiculous.
The parents that God gave you endured tremendous pain and loss.
God blessed them in return with a diamond.
My brother, you are the diamond that I speak of,
Tried and true.
Your progress was a process that was well worth it.
You endured like the true champion that you were.
God preordained you to change the world in a way that's unexplainable.
You took a strong stand against injustice, inequality, and racism.
You said things that no one dared to say.
You described yourself as a "Black Victim" of the system that was not created for Black people.
Your elegance, intelligence, wisdom, charisma, passion, and love for your people were undeniable.
You challenged the status quo, and gave us hope to believe that life can be better for Black people in America and abroad.

William H. Lewis, III

You traveled the world to get a better perspective and understanding that helped you to educate and enlighten your brothers and sisters.

My brother, in the midst of chaos, great challenges, and uncertainty, you displayed unmeasurable resilience, strength, tenacity, and faith.

You were the epitome of discipline, courage, wisdom, and perseverance.

Your legacy is untouchable, unbreakable, and undeniable.

My brother, you were clearly one of the greatest intellectuals of our time.

You did not allow your lack of a formal education to deter you from seeking knowledge and educating yourself in the process.

My brother, thank you for being the great child of God that you were called to be.

Rest in God, my brother!

The one and only, and there will never be another, brother Malcolm X Shabazz.

We love, respect, and appreciate you and the great leadership that you displayed.

Single

I'm highly educated,
I'm extremely humble and loving,
I live alone,
I eat alone,
I go to the movies alone,
I go to the mall alone.
I'm content,
I do get lonely at times,
I love my peace of mind,
I love my freedom,
I date here and there,
I'm not looking for a mate.
I pray every day.
I go to church, most of the time.
I talk to my mom daily.
I talk to my grandparents often.
I never met my father.
I'm the only child.
I do believe in love, thanks to God.

I don't drink,
I don't smoke,
I love ice cream,

William H. Lewis, III

I love going to the beach,
I believe in God whole heartedly.
I look forward to vacations—
I thank God for vacations.
I love children.
I love the elderly.
I like to try new things.
I love myself.
I love to learn about different cultures.
I love life.

Dr. King: A Child of the King of Kings

He was born to be a leader.
He was committed to the grueling task.
He sacrificed so much.
He did not allow fear to interfere.
He believed in justice and equality.
He was a lover and a fighter.
He preached with passion and conviction.
He possessed great knowledge, wisdom, and intellect.
He stepped into his calling with optimism.
He had a dream that's still being realized.
He just wanted to do God's will.
He was made in the image of God.
He gave his life so that we could have a better one.
He knew that his day was coming.
He did not fear any man.
He was not selfish.
He was not hateful.
He was a true man of God.
He did more in 39 years than most of us will do in a lifetime.
Dr. King, thank you for everything!

Solid

He lives alone.
He is God fearing.
He does not have a car.
He rides the bus.
He has never been married.
He loves his mother.
He loves his father.
He has a past that he's not proud of.
He's a hard worker.
He never went to college.
He's loyal.
He's dedicated.
He does not wear fancy clothes.
He loved his grandmother.
He loved his grandfather.
He's not desperate.
He's a true gentleman.
He believes in chivalry.
He's a giver.
He despises injustice.
He hopes to find his queen someday.
He will not settle.
He's very intellectual.

He's very respectful.
He wrestles with demons from the past.
He prays daily,
He has strong faith in God,
He is a true friend.

Finally

I finally passed that test.
I finally got a great job with benefits.
I finally wrote that book.
I finally lost weight.
I finally gained weight.
I finally went on vacation.
I finally got over the flu.
I finally saved enough money to buy a house.
I finally found inner peace.
I finally have time to meditate.
I finally have time to go to the beach.
I finally have time to take my parents out to dinner.
I finally proposed to my girlfriend.
I finally asked her out.
I finally asked him out.
I finally beat cancer.
I finally ran that marathon.
I finally got pregnant.
I finally got my strength back.
I finally went to church.
I finally took time to pray.
I finally gave God some of my time.

I finally made it to school on time.
I finally got that degree.
I finally got my high school diploma.
I finally got enough money to help my family.
I finally saved enough money to buy a car.
I finally took the time to say, "Thank you, Jesus."

Funeral

He transitioned out of this world.
She transitioned out of this world.
The pain and hurt is immeasurable.
The shock and disbelief is heightened.
Crying uncontrollably,
Can't eat,
Can't sleep,
Can't imagine seeing him in a casket,
Can't imagine seeing her in casket,
Sent my condolences through cards, phone calls, and emails.
Can't stand to face his family in person.
Can't stand to face her family in person.
I should have stayed in touch more.
Too late now.
All I have now are distant memories.
I regret not creating new memories.
It's a week later and the body is ready for viewing.
I don't think I'm strong enough to view the body.
How will she look?
How will he look?
God, please give me strength.
God, please give me comfort.
God, please comfort and strengthen every family member and friend.

I finally get enough courage to go to the funeral home.
I walk into this quiet and somber place.
I am escorted to the room where I see her laying in a white casket.
She looks so peaceful.
She's resting.
Her hands are crossed beneath her stomach.
She's recognizable.
Her hair is done so beautifully.
Her dress is beautiful.
Suddenly a deep feeling of emotions take over my body.
I can't stop crying.
I kiss my friend on the cheek.
How sad that she can't kiss me.
She can't hug me.
She can't feel my pain.
He can't feel my pain.
He can't hear my cries.
He is dressed so nicely in his white suit.
I can't ever remember him wearing a suit when he was alive.
I wish I had the chance to see him in a suit when he was alive.
His hair is cut so nicely.
He has white gloves on his hands.
He's recognizable.
I bend over to kiss him on his forehead.
The next day is the funeral.
I arrive at the church.

I see the hearse.
The hearse is the reality.
I walk in the church.
I see the casket in front of the pulpit.
The casket is the reality.
The eulogy is taking place.
The eulogy is over.
The pastor beckons to the funeral directors.
The funeral directors are walking slowly towards the casket.
I can see the stress, anxiety, and anguish of everyone in attendance.
The funeral directors carefully remove the beautiful floral arrangement.
The funeral directors slowly open the casket.
The funeral directors raise the body for viewing.
The church suddenly erupts into cries and praise.
The church hymn, "Going up yonder," is playing as the parting view is taking place.
Thank you, God, for the life that You gave him.
Thank you, God, for the life You gave her.
God has spoken.

A Letter to my Little Black Sister

Little Black Sister, you're beautiful.
Little Black Sister, God loves you unconditionally.
Little Black Sister, put and keep God first in your life.
Little Black Sister, pray every day.
Little Black Sister, I love your hair.
Little Black Sister, I love your skin.
Little Black Sister, you're strong.
Little Black Sister, stay encouraged.
Little Black Sister, you're a natural born leader.
Little Black Sister, never let anyone intimidate you.
Little Black Sister, never-ever give up.
Little Black Sister, express yourself with assertiveness.
Little Black Sister, have no regrets.
Little Black Sister, respect yourself.
Little Black Sister, respect your parents, grandparents, and your guardian.
Little Black Sister, respect your elders.
Little Black Sister, respect your teachers, coaches, mentors, pastors, and all others in authority.

Hard Work

You can never go wrong with hard work.
Hard work is the blue print to success.
It's about working hard all the time.
Even when you feel like slacking, work hard anyway.
Whether at school or work.
Whether in athletics or acting.
Regardless of the situation, work hard.
Work harder than anyone else.
Work until you have nothing else to give.
Model hard work for your children.
Model hard work for your students.
Model hard work for players.
Model hard work for your clients.
Hard work is never wasted.
Hard work always has a purpose.
Hard working people become legendary.
Hard working people are well respected.
Hard working people lead by example.
Hard working people are wired differently.
Hard working people are resilient.
Hard working people never make excuses.

Hard working people will always persevere.
Whatever you lack in talent and skill, hard work will make up for it.
To all of the hard working people in the world, I salute you.

Recidivism

Nothing has changed in my life.
Still living in poverty,
Still impacted by childhood trauma,
Still unemployed,
Still living in the same drug infested neighborhood,
Still dealing with the violent death of my father,
Still dealing with racism,
Still uneducated,
Still illiterate.
Rehabilitation is elusive.
The prison system is a billion dollar corporation.
The system doesn't care about me.
Society doesn't care about me.
I don't even care about me.
This is my normal.
Jail is my normal.
Prison is my normal.
I guess I'll die here.
No one will miss me.

Progress is a Process

Moving forward with a purpose is gratifying.
The moving is never easy.
The steps towards a particular goal requires work.
Keep moving forward.
Don't look back.
Looking back slows you down.
Cooking food requires steps.
Completing college requires action.
But in order to complete something, you have to get started.
Stop thinking about the pain.
Stop thinking about the sleep deprivation.
Stop thinking about the end result.
Prepare yourself for the journey that is necessary.
Prepare yourself for setbacks.
Yes, there will be setbacks.
Don't worry about the setbacks.
Embrace the setbacks.
The setbacks will shape you.
Mindset is crucial.
The right people in your inner circle is crucial.
Trusting in God is extremely crucial.
Trusting in yourself is extremely crucial.
Get ready!

This Day

This day, I will thank God for another opportunity.
This day, I will wake up with a purpose.
This day, I will celebrate small victories.
This day, I will help someone in need.
This day, I will encourage someone to do their best.
This day, I will feed the hungry.
This day, I will pray for the sick.
This day, I will meditate.
This day, I will exercise.
This day, I will eat healthy.
This day, I will show respect to myself and others.
This day, I will have a positive attitude.
This day, I will smile and laugh.
This day, I will keep my mind on God.
This day, I will expect blessings beyond measure.
This day, I will thank God for his past, present, and future blessings.
This day, I will pay my tithes.
This day, I will give an offering.
This day, I will go to church to hear the word of God.
This day, I will hold hands with my neighbors and pray with them.
This day, I will forgive those that have hurt me.

This day, I will forgive myself.
This day, I will show gratitude.
This day, I will show love to my enemies.
This day, I will get on my knees and pray.
This day, I will give it to God.

The Front Row

I have always empathized with families on the front row.
They sit just a few feet away from their loved one, who is finally at peace.
But no matter how loud they talk, scream, cry, or stomp their feet, their loved one cannot hear them.
For their loved one has transitioned from their earthly body to their eternal spirit.
God had spoken because your body was tired.
God had spoken because your purpose was fulfilled.
As supporters and lovers of the bereaved, the pain that they feel does not resonate in the same manner.
Unless the supporters and lovers of the bereaved have experienced a tremendous loss themselves.
Well, up until September 6, 2019, my family was part of the supporter, comforter, prayer, and the call-me-if-you-need-me group.
But on September 6, 2019, my beloved sister, my rock, one of my biggest supporters, one of my biggest cheerleaders, the person that had my back one million percent, transitioned out of this world.
Without question, the most painful and difficult day of my 46 years on this earth.
My soul was crushed!

My spirit broken,
My normal was changed forever.
My only sister in the world silenced forever.
And if that's not a difficult and challenging enough experience consider this:
Reading her death certificate,
Reliving her final moments of life,
Picking out a casket for her,
Choosing an outfit for her to wear,
Viewing her body to make sure that we approved of the preparation,
Viewing her again at her home going service,
Watching them put her body inside of a wall.
Knowing that on September 19, 2019, I would see my sister for the last time.
This is what it mean to be on the front row.
But God said that He would put no more on us than we are able to bear.
I thank God for all of the great memories that I enjoyed with my sister.
I thank God for the not so great memories I endured with my sister.
For it made our love stronger and our faith greater.
Until we meet again, my beloved sister, your spirit will live on through the lives that you touched.
I will love you forever!
God bless you forever, as you have solidified your legacy, Ms. Natasha L. Lewis.

God is Bigger Than...

God is bigger than low self-esteem,
God is bigger than your fears,
God is bigger than your problems,
God is bigger than depression,
God is bigger than anxiety,
God is bigger than drugs,
God is bigger than cigarettes,
God is bigger than vaping,
God is bigger than alcohol,
God is bigger than suicidal ideation,
God is bigger than stress,
God is bigger than poverty,
God is bigger than abuse,
God is bigger than bullying,
God is bigger than racism,
God is bigger than sexism,
God is bigger than bigotry,
God is bigger than broken homes,
God is bigger than illiteracy,
God is bigger than material items,
God is bigger than gentrification,
God is bigger than heartache,

God is bigger than infidelity,
God is bigger than sickness,
God is bigger than hatred,
God is bigger than a college degree,
God is bigger than ineptitude,
God is bigger than privilege,
God is bigger than nightmares,
God is bigger than our yesterday, today, and tomorrow.
God is bigger because He has all power in his hands.
God is bigger because He cannot fail.
God is bigger because He cannot lie.
God is bigger because He is perfect.
God is bigger because He is absolute.
God is bigger because He will never leave, nor forsake us.
God is bigger because He is the end all, be all.
God is bigger because He loves us unconditionally.
God is bigger because His grace is sufficient.
God is bigger because His mercies are many.

Children

One of God's greatest miracles.
One of God's greatest blessings.
Fascinating to say the least.
Intelligent beyond measure.
Intuitive and a zest for life.
Mind blowing and challenging.
Ambitious and independent.
Keeps us honest and on our toes.
Teaches you the true meaning of sleep deprivation.
Will inspire you to be a better person.
Gives us purpose and direction.
Brings us joy and plenty of laughter.
Will make us angry at times.
Will make us sad at times.
Will give us the courage to fight a lion to save their life.
Will make us work harder than ever.
Will make us think before we speak.
Observant and genuine.
Happy and playful.
Will bring out the kid in you.
Future leaders.
Future mentors.
Future teachers.
Future counselors.
Future coaches.

Future prayer warriors.
Future friends and neighbors.
Always God's children.
Thank you, God, for our babies.

The Almighty God-Part 2

Alpha and Omega,
Truth and Life,
Unconditional Lover,
The Ultimate Lover,
The Ultimate Beacon,
The Ultimate Way Maker,
Prince of Peace,
The Ultimate Miracle Worker,
The Giver of Life,
The Giver of Eternal Life,
He First Loved Us,
He Will Always Love Us,
The King of Kings,
The Lord of Lords,
The Greatest Blessing,
Compassionate,
Caring,
Merciful,
Gracious,
Forgiving,
Trustworthy,
Omnipotent,
Omniscient,

From My Heart and Spirit to Yours: A Collection of Poetry

Pure,
Faultless,
Enduring,
Perpetual,
Great,
Always on Time,
Forward Thinker,
Trailblazer,
The One and Only,
Greater than Money,
Greater than Education,
 Greater than Material Items,
 Long-Suffering,
 Teacher,
 Doctor,
 Lawyer,
Creator,
Inventor,
Laborer,
Constant,
Everlasting,
Absolute,
The Same Yesterday,
The Same Today.

A Letter To My Young Black Brothers

YOUNG BLACK BROTHERS, LOVE AND RESPECT YOURSELF.
YOUNG BLACK BROTHERS, EXPRESS YOURSELF DAILY.
YOUNG BLACK BROTHERS, PRAY EVERYDAY.
YOUNG BLACK BROTHERS, TRUST IN GOD.
YOUNG BLACK BROTHERS, TRUST IN YOURSELF.
YOUNG BLACK BROTHERS, DON'T BE CONSUMED BY YOUR PROBLEMS.
YOUNG BLACK BROTHERS, WHEN YOU BECOME OVERWHELMED, GIVE IT TO GOD.
YOUNG BLACK BROTHERS, GOD IS THE BEST THAT YOU CAN EVER HAVE.
YOUNG BLACK BROTHERS, YOU ARE UNIQUE.
YOUNG BLACK BROTHERS, BE THE PERSON GOD MADE YOU TO BE.
YOUNG BLACK BROTHERS, IT'S OKAY TO ASK FOR HELP.
YOUNG BLACK BROTHERS, IT'S OKAY TO CRY.
YOUNG BLACK BROTHERS, NEVER BE AFRAID TO ASK QUESTIONS.
YOUNG BLACK BROTHERS, KNOW YOUR HISTORY.
YOUNG BLACK BROTHERS, DO YOUR OWN RESEARCH.

YOUNG BLACK BROTHERS, STAND STRONG.
YOUNG BLACK BROTHERS, I LOVE YOU.
YOUNG BLACK BROTHERS, I CARE ABOUT YOU.
YOUNG BLACK BROTHERS, MAY GOD BLESS YOU.
YOUNG BLACK BROTHERS, MAY GOD ALWAYS BE YOUR SOURCE OF STRENGTH.
YOUNG BLACK BROTHERS, PLEASE PULL UP YOUR PANTS.

Keep in Touch

Remember your junior high school years?
Remember your high school years?
Remember the last day of school?
Remember when your classmates would write K.I.T in your yearbook?
Some of us actually kept in touch.
Some of us never kept in touch.
Today, we have different ways of keeping in touch.
We have cell phones.
We have Skype.
We have FaceTime.
We have text messaging.
We have voicemail.
We still have good old-fashioned land-line phones.
We still have good old-fashioned answering services.
Unfortunately, in the 21st century, some people have become too busy to communicate with their loved ones.
There are 24 hours in a day.
Take time to call your parents.
Take time to call your grandparents.
Take time to call your siblings.
Take time to call your family members.
Take time to call your friends.

Take time to call someone that you fell out with years ago.
Life is short.
Please don't let death beat you to the punch.
Please remember that the deceased cannot hear you.
The unconscious cannot hear you.
God gave you another day of life.
Do the right thing and call someone.

Make it Right

We used to be best friends.
What happened to our friendship?
You were always there for me;
I was always there for you.
Now we're like strangers.
It hurts me to even say this.
So many years have passed,
I still miss our friendship.
I still miss you.
Let's not let another day pass.
We're not perfect people.
Let's have a conversation.
We can have a conversation.
You're my sister.
You're my brother.
Please forgive me for hurting you.
I love you with all my heart.
Nothing will ever tear us apart.

God is Beyond the Beach

The beach is incredibly massive;
The beach is indicative of God's creativity and infinitude.
The sweet smelling breeze of calm,
The crashing waves that disrupts your normal day,
The slow sailing boat that's moving at a snail's pace across the ocean,
The time in our mind does not compare to God's timetable.
The seagull wants food,
The seagull is very opportunistic,
The beach is the seagull's buffet,
Some people are opportunistic as well.
The ocean water is frigid;
The sun beams across the sand.
One minute you're burning up,
The next minute you're freezing cold.
The beach is the oxymoron of life.
God will allow it,
God wants us to be stable on land and in the water.
God's mercies are many,
God's word is immutable.
The grains of sand represent the many blessings of God, but God's blessings never run out.

The seemingly never ending ocean represents the
    unconditional love of God.
The next time you go to the beach, take a good look at the
    sand.
The next time you go to the beach, take a hard look at the
    infinitude of the ocean.
Though the winds may blow,
The sun will shine.
The shine of the sun is not always a sign of inner peace and
    good vibes.
The brightness may indicate struggle and hardship for some;
Experiences are not the same for everyone.
God has preordained our journey of life.
Stay in your lane.
Stay in your boat.
Stay in your water.
The crashing and the crushing is the shaping and the
    sculpting,
Go through it,
Even if you can't swim, trust God to guide you.
Buried in the sand of debt,
Buried in the sand of abuse,
Buried in the sand of self-hate,
Buried in the sand of divorce,
Buried in the sand of anxiety,

Drowning in the ocean of depression,
Stand still.
Look around you.
Thank God for his past, present, and future blessings.
Thank God for his favor and deliverance.

Give

Give from your heart,
Give with love,
Give with humility,
Give with passion,
Give with understanding,
Give cheerfully,
Give every day.
Give when no one is looking,
Give with compassion,
Give with no regrets,
Be obedient to God when he puts it in your spirit to give.

Be Still

Be still and lift up the name of Jesus.
Be still and know that God is in control.
Be still and stop stressing.
Be still because God has already worked it out.
Be still and rest in the Lord.
Be still and enjoy your family.
Be still and enjoy your food.
Be still and enjoy life.
Be still and bless your brother.
Be still and bless your sister.
Be still and love your neighbor.
Be still and humble yourself.
Be still and smile.
Be still and laugh.
Be still and rejoice.
Be still and don't look back.
Be still and trust in God.
Be still, because God loves you.
Be still, because God knows what you need.
Be still and thank God.
Be still because God is always moving.

God Knows

God is the almighty Father,
God knows your thoughts,
God knows your heart,
God knows your motives,
God knows what you need,
God knows what you don't need,
God knows what's best for you,
God knows about your job situation,
God knows that the rent is due,
God knows your struggles,
God knows your desires,
God knows when you're trusting in Him,
God knows what makes you happy,
God knows what makes you sad.
God knows about your health situation,
God knows everything.

Never Give Up

No matter how it looks,
No matter how far,
No matter how dark,
No matter how tired,
No matter how broke,
No matter how uneducated,
No matter how weak,
No matter how high,
No matter how strong,
No matter how tough,
No matter how big,
No matter how tall,
No matter how small,
No matter how long it will take,
No matter the weather,
No matter the time of day,
No matter if you have a learning disability,
No matter if you grew up in poverty,
No matter if you grew up in foster care,
No matter if you grew up in the hood.
No matter if you grew up in a single parent household,
No matter if you dropped out of school,

William H. Lewis, III

No matter the situation,
Never give up.
Never stop trying.
Never stop trusting God.
Never stop having faith in God.
Never stop believing in yourself.

Impactful

Transitioned, yes, and truly sad to say,
Your life, your love, and your essence was instrumental in shaping me.
I would not be the man that I am without your influence.
Your genuineness and passion for others are unmatched.
Your care and concern was always on full display.
Your warmth and kindness made you lovable.
Your innate ability to nurture children that you didn't birth, was a sign of God in your spirit.
And though you are gone, your love and impact remain.
I will never forget you in this life.
You are a part of my inner being forever.
And, yes, I still cry over your permanent absence.
I long to see that welcoming and pleasant smile.
But I thank God you were in my life during those formative years,
Given the fact we lived in an area that wasn't always so safe.
Thank you for feeding me, when I was hungry.
Thank you for taking me home when it got too late to catch the bus.
Thank you for handing me your son's old school papers and notes, knowing that I could greatly benefit from them.
I know that you loved me.

William H. Lewis, III

I know that you wanted the best for me.
I know that you inquired about me often because that's who you were.

Confined

Will I ever break free from this perpetual state of pain?
I sit behind these bars as a perpetrator and a victim.
Abused and mistreated in my youth.
And love—what is love?
Such a foreign concept to me.
I am still hurting.
My pain is unbearable.
As a result, I have hurt other people.
People have hurt me and showed no mercy in the process.
I did not plan to be this way forever.
I do not like what I see in the mirror.
I see a monster on the outside.
On the inside, I see an eight year old, still screaming for help.
I am sorry for the hurt and pain that I caused.
Please forgive me.
I don't know any better.
I have been judged my entire life.
I often feel cursed.
I do want better for myself.
I can still make a positive difference in the world.
Please don't give up on me.
Please don't throw me away.
Do I still have time?
I am losing hope.
Please pray for me.

www.ingramcontent.com/pod-product-compliance
Lightning Source LLC
Chambersburg PA
CBHW021124080526
44587CB00010B/634